The Muse Among the Motors by Rudyard Kipling

Rudyard Kipling: A great Victorian, a great writer of Empire, a great man.

Rudyard Kipling was one of the most popular writers of prose and poetry in the late 19th and 20th Century and awarded the Noble Prize for Literature in 1907.

Born in Bombay on 30th December 1865, as was the custom in those days, he and his sister were sent back to England when he was 5. The ill-treatment and cruelty by the couple who they boarded with in Portsmouth, Kipling himself suggested, contributed to the onset of his literary life. This was further enhanced by his return to India at age 16 to work on a local paper, as not only did this result in him writing constantly but also made him explore issues of identity and national allegiance which pervade much of his work.

Whilst he is best remembered for his classic children's stories and his popular poem 'If...' he is also regarded as a major innovator in the art of the short story.

Index of Contents

I0158438

Sepulchral

From the Greek Anthologies

Swifter than aught 'neath the sun the car of
    Simonides moved him.
Two things he could not out-run—Death and a
    Woman who loved him.

Arterial

Early Chinese

I

Frost upon small rain—the ebony-lacquered avenue
  Reflecting lamps as a pool shows goldfish.
The sight suddenly emptied out of the young man's eyes
  Entering upon it sideways.

II

In youth, by hazard, I killed an old man.
    In age I maimed a little child.
Dead leaves under foot reproach not:
But the lop-sided cherry-branch—whenever the sun rises,
    How black a shadow!

Carmen Circulare

Q. H. Flaccus

Dellius, that car which, night and day,
  Lightnings and thunders arm and scourge—
Tumultuous down the Appian Way—
  Be slow to urge.
Though reckless Lydia bid thee fly,
  And Telephus o'ertaking jeer,
Nay, sit and strongly occupy
  The lower gear.

They call, the road consenting, "Haste!"—
    Such as delight in dust collected—
Until arrives (I too have raced!)
    The unexpected.
What ox not doomed to die alone,
    Or inauspicious hound, may bring
Thee 'twixt two kisses to the throne
    Of Hades' King,
I cannot tell; the Furies send
    No warning ere their bolts arrive.
'Tis best to reach our chosen end
    Late but alive.

The Advertisement

In the Manner of the Earlier English

Whether to wend through straight streets strictly,
Trimly by towns perfectly paved;
Or after office, as fitteth thy fancy,
Faring with friends far among fields;
There is none other equal in action,
Sith she is silent, nimble, unnoisome,
Lordly of leather, gaudily gilded,
Burgeoning brightly in a brass bonnet,
Certain to steer well between wains.

The Justice's Tale

Chaucer

With them there rode a lustie Engineere
Wel skilled to handel everich waie her geere,
Hee was soe wise ne man colde showe him naught
And out of Paris was hys learnynge brought.
Frontlings mid brazen wheeles and wandes he sat,
And on hys heade he bare an leathern hat.
Hee was soe certaine of his governance,
That, by the Road, he tooke everie chaunce.
For simple people and for lordlings eke
Hee wolde not bate a del but onlie squeeke
Behinde their backés on an horné hie
Until they crope into a piggestie.
He was more wood than bull in china-shoppe,

And yet for cowes and doggés wolde hee stop,
Not out of Marcie but for Preudence-sake—
Than hys dependaunce ever was hys brake.

Done out of Boethius by Geoffrey Chaucer

Blessèd was our first age and morning-time. Then
were no waies tarren, ne no cars numberen, but
each followed his owne playinge-busyness to go
about singly or by large interspaces, for to leden
his viage after his luste and layen under clene
hedge. Jangling there was not, nor the
overtaking wheele, and all those now cruel
clarions were full-hushed and full-still. Then
nobile horses, lest they should make the
chariots moveable to run by cause of this new
feare, we did not press, and were apayed by
sweete thankes of him that drave. There was
not cursings ne adventure of death blinded
bankes betweene, but good-fellowship of
yoke-mates at ignorance equal, and a one pillar of
dust covered all exodus . . . . But, see now how
the blacke road hath strippen herself of hearte
and beauty where the dumbe lampe of Tartarus
winketh red, etc.

Thomas Tusser

Ere stopping or turning, to put foorth a hande
Is a charm that thy daies may be long in the land.
Though seventy-times-seven thee Fortune befriend,
O'ertaking at corners is Death in the end.
Sith main-roads for side-roads care nothing, have care
Both to slow and to blow when thou enterest there.
Drink as thou canst hold it, but after is best;
For Drink with men's Driving makes Crowners to Quest.

Ben Jonson

Love's fiery chariot, Delia, take
Which Vulcan wrought for Venus' sake.
Wings shall not waft thee, but a flame
Hot as my heart—as nobly tame:
Lit by a spark, less bright, more wise
Than linked lightnings of thine eyes!
Seated and ready to be drawn
Come not in muslins, lace or lawn,
But, for thy thrice imperial worth,
Take all the sables of the North,
With frozen diamonds belted on,
To face extreme Euroclydon!
Thus in our thund'ring toy we'll prove
Which is more blind, the Law or Love;
And may the jealous Gods prevent
Our fierce and uncontrouled descent!

The Progress of the Spark

XVIth Circuit

Donne

This spark now set, retarded, yet forbears
To hold her light however so he swears
That turns a metalled crank, and leather cloked,
With some small hammers tappeth hither an yon;
Peering as when she showeth and when is gone;
For wait he must till the vext Power's evoked
That's one with the lightnings. Wait in the showers soaked;
Or by the road-side sunned. She'll not progress.
Poor soul, here taught how great things may by less
Be stayed, to file contacts doth himself address!

The Braggart

Mat. Prior

Petrolio, vaunting his Mercedes' power,
Vows she can cover eighty miles an hour.
I tried the car of old and know she can.

But dare he ever make her? Ask his man!

When the Journey Was Intended to the City

Milton

When that with meat and drink they had fulfilled
Not temperately but like him conceived
In monstrous jest at Meudon, whose regale
Stands for exemplar of Gargantuan greed,
In his own name supreme, they issued forth
Beneath new firmaments and stars astray,
Circumvoluminant; nor had they felt
Neither the passage nor the sad effect
Of many cups partaken, till that frost
Wrought on them hideous, and their minds deceived.
Thus choosing from a progeny of roads,
That seemed but were not, one most reasonable,
Of purest moonlight fashioned on a wall,
Thither they urged their chariot whom that flint
But tressed received, itself unscathed—not they.

To Motorists

Herrick

Since ye distemper and defile
Sweet Herè by the measured mile,
Nor aught on jocund highways heed
Except the evidence of speed;
And bear about your dreadful task
Faces beshrouded 'neath a mask;
Great goblin eyes and glue hands
And souls enslaved to gears and bands;
Here shall no graver curse be said
Than, though y'are quick, that ye are dead!

The Tour

Byron

Thirteen as twelve my Murray always took—

He was a publisher. The new Police
Have neater ways of bringing men to book,
   So Juan found himself before J.P.'s
Accused of storming through that placed nook
   At practically any pace you please.
The Dogberry, and the Waterbury, made
It fifty mile—five pounds. And Juan paid!

The Idiot Boy

Wordsworth

He wandered down the moutain grade
   Beyond the speed assigned—
A youth whom Justice often stayed
   And generally fined.
He went alone, that none might know
   If he could drive or steer.
Now he is in the ditch, and Oh!
   The differential gear!

The Landau

Praed

There was a landau deep and wide,
   Cushioned for Sleep's own self to sit on—
The glory of the country-side
   From Tanner's End to Marlow Ditton.
John of the broad and brandied cheek
    (Well I recall its eau-de-vie hues!)
Drove staid Sir Ralph five days a week
    At speeds which we considered Jehu's . . . .
But now' poor John sleeps very sound,
   And neither hears nor smells the fuss
Of the young Squire's nine-hundred-pound—
   Er—Mors communis omnibus.
And I who in my daily stroll
    Observe the reckless chauffeur crowd her,
Laudator temporis, extol
    The times before the Act allowed her.

Longfellow

The drowsy carrier sways
    To the drowsy horses' tramp.
His axles winnow the sprays
Of the hedge where the rabbit plays
    In the light of his single lamp.
He hears a roar behind,
    A howl, a hoot, and a yell,
A headlight strikes him blind
And a stench o'erpowers the wind
    Like a blast from the mouth of Hell.
He mends his swingle-bar,
    And loud his curses ring;
But a mother watching afar
Hears the hum of the doctor's car
    Like the beat of an angel's wing!
So, to the poet's mood,
    Motor or carrier's van,
Properly understood,
Are neither evil nor good—
    Ormuzd not Ahriman!

Tennyson

This is the end whereto men toiled
    Before thy coachman guessed his fate—
    How thou shouldst leave thy, 'scutcheoned gate
On that new wheel which is the oiled—
To see the England Shakespeare saw
    (Oh, Earth, 'tis long since Shallow died!
    Yet by yon farrowed sow may hide
Some blue deep minion of the Law)—
To range from Ashby-de-la-Zouch
    By Lyonnesse to Locksley Hall,
    Or haply, nearer home, appal
Thy father's sister's staid barouche.

After He Has Been Extemporising on an Instrument Not of His Own Invention

Browning

Lo! What is this that I make—sudden, supreme, unrehearsed—
    This that my clutch in the crowd pressed at a venture has raised?
Forward and onward I sprang when I thought (as I ought) I reversed,
    And a cab like martagon opes and I sit in the wreckage dazed.
And someone is taking my name, and the driver is rending the air
    With cries for my blood and my gold, and a snickering news-boy brings
My cap, wheel-pashed from the kerb. I must run her home for repair,
    Where she leers with her bonnet awry—flat on the nether springs!

Lady Geraldine's Hardship

E.B. Browning

I turned— Heaven knows we women turn too much
To broken reeds, mistaken so for pine
That shame forbids confession—a handle I turned
(The wrong one, said the agent afterwards)
And so flung clean across your English street
Through the shrill-tinkling glass of the shop-front—paused,
Artemis mazed 'mid gauds to catch a man,
And piteous baby-caps and christening-gowns,
The worse for being worn on the radiator.

My cousin Romney judged me from the bench:
Propounding one sleek forty-shillinged law
That takes no count of the Woman's oversoul.
I should have entered, purred he, by the door—
The man's retort—the open obvious door—
And since I chose not, he—not he—could change
The man's rule, not the Woman's, for the case.
Ten pounds or seven days . . . Just that . . . I paid!

The Bother

Clough

Hastily Adam our driver swallowed a curse in the darkness—
Petrol nigh at end and something wrong with a sprocket
Made him speer for the nearest town, when lo! at the crossways

Four blank letterless arms the virginal signpost extended.
"Look!" thundered Hugh the Radical. "This is the England we boast of—
Bland, white-bellied, obese, but utterly useless for business.
They are repainting the signs and have left the job in the middle.
They are repainting the signs and traffic may stop till they've done it,
Which is to say: till the son-of-a-gun of a local contractor,
Having laboriously wiped out every name for
Probably thirty miles round, be minded to finish his labour!
Had not the fool the sense to paint out and paint in together?"
Thus, not seeing his speech belied his Radical Gospel
(Which is to paint out the earth and then write "Damn" on the shutter),
Hugh embroidered the theme imperially and stretched it
From some borough in Wales through our Australian possessions,
Making himself, reformer-wise, a bit of a nuisance
Till, with the help of Adam, we cast him out on the landscape.

The Dying Chauffeur

Adam Lindsay Gordon

Wheel me gently to the garage, since my car and I must part—
   No more for me the record and the run.
That cursèd left-hand cylinder the doctors call my heart
   Is pinking past redemption—I am done!
They'll never strike a mixture that'll help me pull my load.
   My gears are stripped—I cannot set my brakes.
I am entered for the finals down the timeless untimed Road
   To the Maker of the makers of all makes!

The Inventor

R. W. Emerson

Time and Space decreed his lot,
   But little Man was quick to note:
When Time and Space said Man might not,
   Bravely he answered, "Nay! I mote."
I looked on old New England.
   Time and Space stood fast.
Men built altars to Distance
   At every mile they passed.
Yet sleek with oil, a Force was hid
Making mock of all they did,
Ready at the appointed hour
   To yield up to Prometheus

The secular and well-drilled Power
　　The Gods secreted thus.
And over high Wantastiquer
　　Emulous my lightnings ran,
Unregarded but afret,
　　To fall in with my plan.
I beheld two ministries,
　　One of air and one of earth—
At a thought I married these,
　　And my New Age came to birth!
For rarely my purpose errs
　　Though oft it seems to pause,
And rods and cylinders
　　Obey my planets' laws.
Oil I drew from the well,
　　And Franklin's spark from its blue;
Time and Distance fell,
　　And Man went forth anew.
On the prairie and in the street
　　So long as my chariots roll
I bind wings to Adam's feet,
　　And, presently, to his soul!

Wardour Street Border Ballad

"Now this is the price of a stirrup-cup,"
　　The kneeling doctor said.
And syne he bade them take him up,
　　For he saw that the man was dead.
They took him up, and they laid him down
　　(And, oh, he did not stir),
And they had him into the nearest town
　　To wait the Coroner.
They drew the dead-cloth over the face,
　　They closed the doors upon,
And the cars that were parked in the market-place
　　Made talk of it anon.
Then up and spake a Daimler wide,
　　That carries the slatted tank:—
"'Tis we must purge the country-side
　　And no man will us thank.
"For while they pray at Holy Kirk
　　The souls should turn from sin,
We cock our bonnets to the work,

And gather the drunken in.—
"And if we spare them for the nonce—
    Or their comrades jack them free—
They learn more under our dumb-iròns
    Than they learned at time mother's knee."
Then up and spake an Armstrong bold,
    And Siddeley, was his name:—
"I saw a man lie stark and cold
    By Grantham as I came.
"There was a blind turn by a brook,
    A guard-rail and a fail:
But the drunken loon that overtook
    He got no hurt at all!
"I ha' trodden the wet road and the dry—
    But and the shady lane;
And why the guiltless soul should die,
    Good reason find I nane."
Then up and spake the Babe Austin—
    Had barely room for two—
"'Tis time and place that make the sin,
    And not the deed they do.
"For when a man drives with his dear,
    I ha' seen it come to pass
That an arm too close or a lip too near
    Has killed both lad and lass.
"There was a car at eventide
    And a sidelings kiss to steal—
The God knows how the couple died,
    But I mind the inquest weel.
"I have trodden the black tar and the heath—
    But and the cobble-stone;
And why the young go to their death,
    Good reason find I none."
Then spake a Morris from Oxenford,
    ('Was keen to a Cowley Friar):—
"How shall we judge the ways of the Lord
    That are but steel and fire?
"Between the oil-pits under earth
    And the levin-spark from the skies,
We but adventure and go forth
    As our man shall devise:
"And if he have drunken a hoop too deep,
    No kinship can us move
To draw him home in his market-sleep
    Or spare his waiting love.
"There is never a lane in all England
    Where a mellow man can go,
But he must look on either hand

And back and front also.
"But he must busk him every tide,
    At prick of horn, to leap
Either to hide in ditch beside
    Or in the bankès steep.
"And whether he walk in drink or muse,
    Or for his love be bound,
We have no wit to mark and chuse,
    But needs must slay or wound."

They drew the dead-cloth from its face.
    The Crowner looked thereon;
And the cars that were parked in the market-place
    Went all their ways anon.

A Child's Garden

R. L. Stevenson

Now there is nothing wrong with me
Except—I think it's called T.B.
And that is why I have to lay
Out in the garden all the day.
Our garden is not very wide,
And cars go by on either side,
And make an angry-hooty noise
That rather startles little boys.
But worst of all is when they take
Me out in cars that growl and shake,
With charabancs so dreadful-near
I have to shut my eyes for fear.
But when I'm on my back again,
I watch the Croydon aeroplane
That flies across to France, and sings
Like hitting thick piano-strings.
When I am strong enough to do
The things I'm truly wishful to,
I'll never use a car or train
But always have an aeroplane;
And just go zooming round and round,
And frighten Nursey with the sound,
And see the angel-side of clouds,
And spit on all those motor-crowds!

Author Unknown

You mustn't groom an Arab with a file.
 You hadn't ought to tension-spring a mule.
You couldn't push a brumby fifty mile
 And drop him in a boiler-shed to cool.
I'll sling you through six counties in a day.
 I'll hike you up a grade of one in ten.
I am Duty, Law and Order under way,
 I'm the Mentor of banana-fingered men!
I will make you I know your left hand from your right.
 I will teach you not to drink about your biz.
I'm the only temperance advocate in sight!
 I am all the Education Act there is!

PREFACE BY SAMUEL JOHNSON

It is to be observed of this play that, though its plan is irregular, it has been made instrumental to the production of many discriminate characters who deliver themselves with candour and propriety, as they approach towards, or recede from, the operations of Justice. The juxtaposition of Hamlet and Falstaff may be questioned by the learned or the delicate, but the conjectural critic of an author neither systematic nor consequential can affirm that those same forces of natural genius, which expatiate in splendour and passion, demand for their refreshment and sanity an abruptness of release and a lawlessness of invention, proportioned to precedent constrictions. He only who hath never toiled in the anfractuous mines of Philosophy or Letters, nor subdued himself to the ignoble needs of the Stage, will dispute the proposition.

There is a tradition that this play was composed after a drinking bout. I would prefer to credit that it owed its birth to some such concatenation of circumstances as (1) have adumbrated. The more so since, amid much that is ill-considered, or even depraved, our author has assigned to the crafty and careless Falstaff an awful, if fleeting, visitation of self-knowledge. Let us now be told no more of the illegitimacy of this play

ACT I

Argument, **FALSTAFF**, **NYM**, **POINS**, **BARDOLPH** and **FLUELLEN** having accompanied **PRINCE HENRY** in a motor drive through the city of London, their car breaks down, and **FALSTAFF** returns to the Boar's Head Tavern in Eastcheap, where he is, followed by the **PRINCE** and **FLUELLEN**.

[Enter **FALSTAFF**, habited as a motorist

Here's all at an end between us, or I'll never taste sack again. Prince or no Prince, I'll not ride with him to Coventry on the hinder parts of a carbonadoed stink, not though he call her all the car in Christendom. Sack! Sack! Sack!

HOSTESS
I spied her out of the lattice. A' fizzled and a' groaned and a' shook from the bones out, Sir John, and a' ran on her own impulsidges back and forth o' Chepe, and I knew that there was but one way to it when I saw them fighting at the handles. She died of a taking of pure wind on the heart, and they be about her body now with tongs. A marvellous searching perfume, Sir John!

FALSTAFF
He hath called me ribs; he hath called me tallow. There is no name in the extremer oiliness of comparisons which I have not borne meekly. But to go masked at midday; to wrap my belly in an horse-hide cloak of ten thousand buttons till I looked like a mushroomed dunghill; to be smoked over burnt oils; to be enseamed, moreover, with intolerable greases; and thus scented, thus habited, thus vizarded, to leap out-for I leaped, mark you . . . Another cup of sack! But there's vengeance for my case! These eyes have seen the Lord's Anointed on his knees in Chepe, foining with the key of Shrewsbury Castle, which Poins had bent to the very crook of Nym's theftuous elbow, to wake the dumb devil in the guts of her. "Sweet Hal," said I, "are all horses sold out of England, that thou must kneel before the lieges to any petrol-piddling turnspit?" Then he, Poins, and Bardolph whose nose blanched with sheer envy of her bodywork, begged a shoulder of me to thrust her into some alley, the street being full of Ephesians of the old church. Whereat I . . .

[Enter **PRINCE** and **FLUELLEN**

PRINCE
Whereat thou, hearing her once or twice tenderly backfire—

FALSTAFF
Heaven forgive thee, Hal! She thundered and lightened a full half-hour, so that Jove Himself could not have bettered the instruction. There's a pit beneath her now, which she blew out of thy father's highway the while I watched, where Sackerson could stand to six dogs.

PRINCE
Hearing, I say, her gentle outcry against Poins' mishandling, thou didst flee up Chepe, calling upon the Sheriff's Watch for a red flag.

FALSTAFF
I? Call me Jack if I were not jack to each of her wheels in turn till I am stamped like a butter-pat with the imprint of her underpinnings. I seek a red flag?

PRINCE
Ay, roaring like a bull.

FALSTAFF
Groans, Hal, groans such as Atlas heaved. But she overbore me at. the last. Why hast thou left her?—Faugh, that a King's son should ever reek like a smutty-wicked lamp upon the wrong side of the morning!

PRINCE

There was Bardolph in the buckbasket behind, nosing fearfully overside like a full-wattled turkey-poult from Norfolk. There was Poins upon his belly beneath her, thrice steeped in pure plumbago, most despairfully clanking of chains like the devil in Brug's Hall window; and there were some four thousand 'prentices at her tail, crying, "What ho!" and that she bumped. Methought 'twas no place for my father's son.

FALSTAFF

Take any man's horses and hale her to bed! The laws of England are at thy commandment, that the Heir should not be made a common stink in the nostrils of the lieges.

PRINCE

She'd not stir for all Apollo's team—not though Phæton himself, drunk with nectar, lashed 'em stark mad. Poor Phæton!

HOSTESS

A' was a King's son, was a' not, and came to's end by keeping of bad company?

FALSTAFF

No more than a little horseflesh. I tell thee, Hal, this England of ours has never looked up since the nobles fell to puking over oil-buckets by the side of leather-jerkined Walloons.

PRINCE

He that drives me now is French as our princely cousin.

FALSTAFF

Dumain? Hang him for a pestilent, poke-eyed, chicken-chopping, hump-backed, leather-hatted, muffle-gloved ape! He hath been fined as often as he hath broken down; and that is at every tavern 'twixt here and York. Dumain! He's the most notorious widow-maker on the Windsor road. His mother was a corn-cutter at Ypres, and his father a barber at Rouen, by which beastly conjunction he rightly draws every infirmity that damns him in his trade. Item: He cuts corners niggardly and upon the wrong side. Item: He'll look behind him after a likely wench in the hottest press of Holborn, though he skid into the kennel for it. Item: He depends upon his brake to save him at need—a death-bed repentance, Hal, as hath been proved ere this, since grace is uncertain. Item: He is too proud to clean the body of her, but leaves the care of that which should be the very cote-armour of his mechanic knighthood to an unheedful ostler. Thus, at last, he comes to overlook even the oiling; and so it falls that she's where she must be, and not where thou wouldst have her. Ay, laugh if thou wilt, Hal, but a round worthy knight need not fire himself through three baronies in eight hours to know the very essence of the petrol1 that fumes him. Domain will one day clutch thee into Hell upon the first speed.

PRINCE

Strange that clear knowledge should so long outlive mere nerve! I'll dub Domain knight when I come to the throne, if he be not hanged first for murder on the highway. 'Twill save the state a pension.

FALSTAFF

So the lean vice goes ever before the solid virtue,—
[Confused noise without]

What riot's afoot now?

FLUELLEN
Riots, look you, by my vizaments, make one noise, but murders another. There's riots in Monmouth; but, by my vizaments, look you, there's murders in Chepe. Pabes and old 'oomen—they howl so tamnably.

FALSTAFF
Rebellion rather! Half London's calling on thy name, Hal, and half on thy father's. Well, if it be successful, forget not who was promised the reversion of the Chief Justice-ship. Ha! Unquestioned rebellion, if broken crowns signify aught.

[Enter **HERALDS**, wounded.

Most gracious lord, the car that bore thy state,
Too long neglected and adjudged acold,
Hath, without warning or advertisement,
Risen refreshed from her supposed stand
In unattended revolution.

PRINCE
This it is to be a King's son! That a pitiful twelve horse touring-car(2) cannot jar off her brakes but they must rehearse it me in damnable heroics. Your pleasure, gentlemen?

HERALDS
The blood upon our boltered brow attests
'Twas Bardolph's art that waked her, whereat she
Skipped thunderously before our mazèd eyes,
Drew out o'er several lieges (all with God!),
Battered a house or so to lathes, and now
Fumes on her side in Holborn. Please you, come!

PRINCE
Anon! Seek each a physician according to his needs and revenues. I'll be with you anon.
[To **FALSTAFF**]
The third in three weeks! These whoreson German clockcases no sooner dint honest English paving-stone than they incontinent lay their entrails on the street. Five hundred and seventy pounds! I'll out and pawn the Duchy!

HERALDS
The Lord Chief Justice waits thy princely will,
In thy dread father's Court at Westminster.

FALSTAFF
A Star Chamber matter, Hal—a Star Chamber matter! Glasses, Doll! We'll drink to his deliverance.

HERALDS
You, too, Sir John, as party to those broils

And breakings-forth, in like attainder stand
For judgment: wherein fail not at your peril!

FALSTAFF
I do remember now to have had some dealings with this same Chief Justice. An old feeble man, drawn abroad in a cart by horses. We must enlighten—enlighten him, Hal.

[Exeunt.

ACT II

Argument. **PRINCE HENRY, POINS, FLUELLEN, NYM,** and **SIR JOHN FALSTAFF** [**BARDOLPH** having escaped] are charged, on **DOGBERRY'S** evidence, before the **LORD CHIEF JUSTICE** at Westminster, with exceeding the speed-limit and leaving their car unattended in the street. **PORTIA** defends them. **JUSTICE SHALLOW** has been accommodated with a seat on the Bench.

PRINCE
Where's our red rear-lamp? Where's Bardolph?

POINS
Shining over Southwark if he be not puffed out by now. He ran when the watch came. The Chief Justice looks sourly. Is any appointed to speak for us, Hal?

PRINCE
Thy notorious innocence, my known virtue, and if these fail, Sir John's big belly. I have fed my father's exchequer here twice since Easter.

CHIEF JUSTICE
Intemperate, rash, and ill-advisèd men—
Yoke-fellows at unsavoury enterprise—
Harry, and you, Sir John, stand forth for sentence!

FLUELLEN
Put—put there is no indictments discharged upon us yet. To pronounce sentences, look you, pefore the indictments is discharged is ropperies and oppressions.

NYM
Ay, that's the humour of it. When they cry Budget we must cry mum.

FALSTAFF
Cram the Welsh flannel down his own throat, or we are imprisoned after the fine. I know the Chief Justice is sick of me.

SHALLOW [To **CHIEF JUSTICE**]
My lord, my lord, if you suffer yon fat knight to talk, he'll cozen the teeth out of your lord-ship's head, while his serving-man steals the steeped crust you'd mumble to. I lent him a thousand pounds, my lord.

FALSTAFF
I deny it not. For the which I promised thee advancement. And art thou not now visibly next the Chief justice himself?

SHALLOW
Not on my merits, Sir John. I sit here simple of courtesy as visiting-justice. I'd do as much for my lord if he came to Gloucestershire, 'faith!

FALSTAFF
Shallow! Shallow! I say I gave thee occasion and opportunity to rise. Promotion is in thy hands.
[To **CHIEF JUSTICE**]
Have a care, my lord! He fingers his dagger already.

SHALLOW
My dagger? My ink-horn, la! I'll sit further off. I told you how he'd talk, my lord. But I'll sit further off. My dagger, 'faith!

CHIEF JUSTICE
Sir John! Sir John! The licence of inveterate humour overstretched rends like an outworn garment—with like shame to the enduer. Answer me roundly, what defence make you to the charge you have run through Chepe at ten leagues the hour?

FALSTAFF
Roundly, my lord, my shape—my evident shape.

CHIEF JUSTICE
But 'tis so charged, and will be so witnessed.

DOGBERRY
Yes, and by one that hath a stopped watch and everything forsworn about him. Write it down fifteen leagues, my lord.

PRINCE [To **CHIEF JUSTICE**]
We knights of the road have ever been fair quarry for your knights of the post to bind to, but this passes endurance. We left our car, my lord, extinct and combust in the kennel, while we sought an engineer to hoist her. In which stay she would have continued, but for the prying vulgar who found on her some handle to their curiosity, which, doubtless, they turned. For in such a car as this—

CHIEF JUSTICE
In such a car as this
The enfranchised 'prentices of London quash
Our harmless babes and necessary wives
At morning to the sound of Sabbath bells
Through panicked Huntingdon.

PORTIA
In such a car as this,
Slides young Desire athwart the mountain-tops,

Drinking the airs that part him from his dear
'Twixt Berwick and Glamorgan.

CHIEF JUSTICE
In such a car as this,
The lecherous Israelite to Brighthelmstone
Convoys his Jessica.

PORTIA
In such a car as this,
The lean chirurgeon burns the midnight oil
Impetuous over England. Where his lamp
Strikes pale the hedgerow, all the affrighted fays,
Their misty revels in the dew divulged,
Flee to the coney's burrow, or divide
His antre with the squirrel—whom that ministrant
Marks not, his eyes being bent to thrid the dark,
Indifferent beneath the morning star,
To the poor cot that summoned him, and the life—
Some hour-old, mother-naked life, scarce held
By the drowsy midwife but it yarks and squeaks
Batlike, and batlike, would to the void again.
This he forbids, and yet not he, whose art,
His car unaiding, else had ne'er o'erleaped
The largess of a county in an hour.

SHALLOW
Neat, faith, la! For how a brace of twins now, the far side Cotsall, of a snowy night, my lord?

FALSTAFF
A pregnant wit. Which of thy misdeeds, Hal, hath raised this angel to help us? I'll ask Doll.

PRINCE
Peace, dunghill, peace! She was never of Doll's company.

PORTIA
And I charge you, my lord, if ever need,
Extreme and urgent need, hath visited you,
Or, in the unprobeable decree of Time,
May visit and masterfully constrain, think well
Ere your abhorrence of new enginery
Seal up the avenues of mercy here!

CH. JUSTICE
I sealed no avenues. They sealed the King's
(Albeit it was called Northumberland)
With hellish engines drawn across the street
In an opposed and desperate barrier

Unto the lieges' progress.

PORTIA
Not by their will, nor their intent, my lord!
It was a passing humour of the car
Gusty incontinence which, overlooked,
As unregard oft cows pretension,
May well not chance again.

CHIEF JUSTICE
But if it chance?

PORTIA
If the deep-brooding vault of Heaven retain
Memory and record of miracle
Vouchsafed, like this your prayed-for mercy, once,
And, in default of quail, rain from her gate
Heaven's sweetest choristers—then it may fall,
But not till then!

FLUELLEN
Put—put—look you, she is telling the old shentlemans to wait till the sky shall rain larks! It is open contempts of Courts!

NYM
Ay, there's humours in them all. But I think the old man's humour is sweeter.

CHIEF JUSTICE
Yet, bating miracle, how if mercy breed
Not gratitude, but livelier insolence,
And through my softened verdict after years
Grow bold to break the law? How if our England—
Loverly, temperate, the midmost close of peace—
Dissolve in smoke and oils along the green,
Till sickened memory conceive no minute
Unharried, unpollutable, unhooted?
If I loose these, what do I loose on England?

PORTIA
Too late! Too late! That babe is viable!
The hour we dread o'ertops us while we wonder,
Not asking sufferance, but imposing change,
Most multitudinously. Hark, it sings i' the wind!

ARIEL [Invisible] sings
    Where the car slips there slip I—
    In a sunbeam's path I lie!
    There I crouch while crowds do cry,

After somersaults muddily!
Where I lie, where I lie, shall I live now
Under the bonnet that bangs on my brow?

FALSTAFF [To **PRINCE**]
The Chief Justice is mazed by the fairies. He hath great motions towards virtue. He'll let us go.

CHIEF JUSTICE
Ourselves have snuffed some savour of these changes,
And more our horses who, poor winkered fools,
Hearing their dooms outstrip them, cast aside
And pole the all-shattered house-fronts.
                                    We ourselves,
Of purpose to repair to Westminster,
Infirmity and age consenting, signalled
From her hot lair an horseless chariot
Which, in the recorded twelfth part of an hour,
Bore our inviolate ermines half a league.
It is, and woe it is, the chill refuge,
The lean, unenvied privilege of Age,
To meet new changes with old courtesy,
Not as averting change but sparing souls
Worn weak, and bodies extenuate with the years
That heed nor never heeded! Set them free.
What has been was, and what will be, must be!

ACT III

Argument. A room in the Boar's Head Tavern set for a banquet to celebrate the discharge of the motorists from the King's justice. Enter **PRINCE HENRY** with **PORTIA** and several others. Also **FALSTAFF** drunk.

FALSTAFF
"When that I had and a little tinny car—
With a heigh-ho, the wind and the screen—"
Empty the radiator!

HOSTESS
Sir John, there's one without says he's your twin brother.

FALSTAFF
I'll be the wise child. Have him in!
[Enter **HAMLET** drunk]
Ha! 'Begot a night's ride the cooler side o' the blanket! But if I be knight, . . he's Blood-Royal.
[To **PRINCE HENRY**]
Here's thy meat, Hal. I stay by our commons.

PRINCE
Lions know lions, tho' they pride apart,
And Princes Princes.
[To **HAMLET**]
For these, my companions
Rejoicingly from Justice, your pardon, Brother,
And, if it so far please, your title.

HAMLET
Prince. Hamlet of Denmark. Your pardon too. 'Tis the Rhenish . . . But conceive, sirrah, how it comes about 'neath the unjust stars, that by a few ink-spirts and frail pretences of the plays, a bald-paced ostler to Pegasus conjures life into such as we. In which continuance, mark you, we live and inextinguishably shake spheres: he having left the globe—how long? But I'll go find my double.(3)

PRINCE
Rumour wrongs not the Danes. They drink too deep.
He is full proof.
[To **HAMLET**]
Welcome, distracted Sir.
We have a foolish feast in hand, whereat,
Wine and our near escapes making familiar,
You shall be richer by a score of brothers
Before the score is paid. Seek and make merry.
[To **NYM**]
When the fat gentleman stumbles, lay him against the arras, head highest. There's a crown waiting.

NYM
For him—not me. That's an old humour.

PRINCE [To **PORTIA**]
'Lovely lady,
To whom we go in bondage, first, of beauty,
And next of golden advocacy, snatching
Us from deservèd Bridewells—name thy fee.

PORTIA
I here confess I never owned a car;
Never, in all my life, have driven car;
And, touching any uses of a car,
From airiest hearsays (4) were my pleadings drawn.
Therefore, I ask no guerdon but a car,
To experience on the heels of phantasy.

PRINCE
A car? A car?

PORTIA
I said even so—one car.

HAMLET [To **FALSTAFF**]
Women have dread affections, for their spirit,
Out-plumbing ours, their easier sympathies
Frame both the passion and the appurtenance;
Else they go mad.

FALSTAFF
True! Doll's a she-kite of the same feather. But moulting—moulting!

PRINCE [To **PORTIA**]
Nay, entertain conjecture of a time
When, horses fed to hounds, the thrice-stuffed streets
Ring, reek and rumble with opprobrious wains
Inveterately unheedful. Straw between
Their bulks the rash and pillioned amorists
Whose so mis-timed embracernents on the wood (5)
Sling hose and cap (6) to inquest.

BEATRICE
Signor Prince, spare thyself a dry mouth and us drier discourse. The world moves, for all man's owlings, and we women in the va'ward (7).

NYM
That's the new humour. To over-run the law and the lieges and say "I am a maid!"

BENEDICK
To have at a man sideways out of a blind lane, and if he give natural vent on some broken head, arm, or running board (8), her husband or lover must challenge him as though he were Claudio.

BEATRICE
That, Signor Benedick, shall never be. For when I drive you shall stay at home.

SHYLOCK
I have a bond! I have a bond in my office,
Whose virtue is—for every pound of flesh,
Or drop of blood, on such mistakings drawn,
Or push of market-bestial—being signed
(And some poor ducats paid) assures the holder
'Gainst every act and charge of law or leech.

PORTIA
We made sweet composition long ago,
Shylock and I. He pays upon such bonds,
As, in mine office, I can well avouch;
Having prepared the like for Jessica
Whose paths are wayward. Let them see it, Jew.

[**SHYLOCK** shows the company a Third Party Risks Policy. **HAMLET** and **FALSTAFF** talk apart]

FALSTAFF [To **HAMLET**]
Unconfined truth! Cowards natural, both of us, with each some huddled deliverance of jest or philosophy to piece out the skirts of 'voided occasion. 'You drive?

HAMLET
For action to be taken on the instant? I'd liever . . .! But, oh, God—I have no choice, being what I am and informed of myself past endurance.

FALSTAFF
I have some same cause. How, now, of drink and lechery to drown self-knowledge?

HAMLET
'Serves me not. There's a mad woman whom I drowned floats in my every cup, like borage (9). But I am not brave.

FALSTAFF
Women in liquor! Double damnation and half satisfaction. Think you, Ham, that he who made us twins knew his work?

HAMLET
I set no limit, being born of that soul—
One spark in all its hells. Flesh, canst thou tremble?

FALSTAFF
I am too young to 'scape the cold fit o' mornings.

HAMLET
Shake to thy core, contemplating what vasts
Unlawful, and what darkness, whereto ours
Is the sun's targe, had he adventured down
(Holding the poised brain ice) till he arraigned (10)
A murderess, a Moor, a mad King—me!
For ensample of all uttermosts of woe
Man bears or shall be designate to suffer
Inly or of the Gods!

FALSTAFF
True enough. But the sack's here, and I have 'scaped Justice an hour. What a plague does the Jew with his papers?

PRINCE [Taking Insurance Policy from **SHYLOCK**]
Thus furnished, and with knowledge of the wealth
Behind the bond, are all my doubts resolved.
My fears? [To **PORTIA**] Fair lady, warn me of thy comings
When that car rolls its fifty roystering steeds
Which is our instant, grateful, deadly gift!

SIR A. AGUECHEEK

There's simply no back-alley left in Illyria now where a man may let's liquor out of him, but he must stand ready to leap into either hedge.

PRINCE

To-morrow be his own klaxon (11). Till he call,
Put cars away, and revel comrades all!

FESTE

When all about the joiners thrive—
    And coffins quick as man can saw;—
When learning lady-owners drive,
    And beaks sit brooding on the Law;
When roasting cabs hiss on the grass,
Then lightly brays the headlong ass:—
    "Where to? To Hell!" Oh, word of fear,
Unpleasing to the charioteer!

FOOTNOTES

1. *Petard, which is almost synonymous. HORNE TOOKE: First Folio: private notes upon.*

2. *Touraine-cart (conjectural).—WARBURTON.*

3. *. . . . After the transparent reference to "the unjust stars," the word "inkspirts" leaps to the eye of the initiated as the simplest anagram of "scripsit" (the "k" being used, of course, for the desiderated "c," and the apparently superfluous "n," for the initial of Nicholas, Bacon's father). "Frail pretences" (taking the first three letters of the first, and the last four of the second, word) reveals, beyond negation, the same "Frances" who wrote to his King (Mar. 25, 1631) that he might be "frail and partake, etc." The "bald-pated ostler" who "conjures life into, etc.," is even more palpable and needs not the addi tional "continuance" which follows. Nor does this exhaust the category. Miss Nessa Droenbergh acutely explains Hamlet's opening remark to Prince Henry as a well-bred man's apology for phenomena due to liquor-excess—briefly a hiccough. But we must remember that Bacon, where possible, always "doubles his clues," on the principle of the British railroads' "distant" and "home" signals. Thus after "Your pardon too," comes "'Tis the Rhenish," a German wine long traded into Britain and the Baltic, and later known as "hoc(k)." So we have, all but en clair, the author of "Shakespeare's" plays proclaiming, "Hoc scripsit Frances Bacon." (Francis Bacon wrote this.) What more, in the name of sanity, is needed to convince anyone who is not delivered over to the "man of Stratford" complex?—From PROFESSOR O. P. CALLOWITZ'S William the World-Impostor.*

4. *Hearses.—WARBURTON (conjectural).*

5. *The text is corrupt. It is impossible to imagine a street paved with wood. But mis-timed embracements might well be "untoward."— JOHNSON.*

6. At this epoch the London 'prentices wore cloth caps, and their female companions stockings, which had then been largely discovered by the vulgar.—THEOBALD.

7. "Ford" (conjectural).—STEEVENS.

8. 'Running aboard—in the sense of vessels falling "foul" of each other at sea, (Conjectural.)— JOHNSON.

9. An allusion to the old distich:

> "I, Borage,
> Give courage."

The herb is not included in the Queen's category of those used by Ophelia previous to her suicide, nor does Ophelia herself mention it. (Conjectural.)— STEEVENS.

10. Mr. Malone says that this word should be "arrayed," in the sense of displaying before the public; but considering that each one of the characters enumerated is, in various forms, arraigned by Conscience, that most dreadful of judges, I incline towards the former reading.—M. MASON.

11. "Sexton." This word, through corruption, has been lost, and is now restored to its original meaning.— SIR T. HANMER.

Rudyard Kipling – A Short Biography

Born in Bombay on 30th December 1865, Joseph Rudyard Kipling wrote short stories, poems and novels, a body of work whose reputation is in constant flux as his presentations and interpretations of empire are viewed within the changing context of empirical absolution in the twentieth century. Having spent the first five years of his life in India he felt a natural affinity for the country, though his upbringing had a distinctly colonial taste flavour. He was born in the Bombay Presidency of British India to Lockwood Kipling, an English art teacher and illustrator who took a position as professor of architectural sculpture in the Jeejeebhoy School of Art and Alice MacDonald, spoken of by the a Viceroy of India that "dullness and Mrs Kipling cannot exist in the same room". Though their presence in India was principally artistic and educational, rather than political, the company they kept and the establishments in which they kept it indicate an existence very much benefitting from the British Empire. Lockwood would later go on to assume a position as curator of the Lahore Museum, while working on various illustrations for Rudyard's writing, and various decorations for the Victoria and Albert museum in London. Much of his work, then, was coloured by the empire, whether in service to or benefitting from, and it was into this distinctly British experience of India that Rudyard was born.

Lockwood and Alice had met and fallen in love at Rudyard Lake in Rudyard, Staffordshire, and their affections for the area were so great they chose to refer to the lake in naming their first-born. Alice came from a family of four sisters, all of whose marriages were significant and well-arranged; moreover, Rudyard's most famous relative was Stanley Baldwin, Conservative Prime Minister on three occasions in the 1920s and 1930s. Kipling's sense of belonging in Bombay is found in 'To the City of Bombay' in the dedication to Seven Seas, a collection of poems published in 1900, which reads:—

Mother of Cities to me,
For I was born in her gate,
Between the palms and the sea,
Where the world-end steamers wait.

His parents considered themselves Anglo-Indians, and he would later assume this classification although he did not live there long. His first five years, which he describes as days of "strong light and darkness", ended when he and his three-year-old sister Alice were removed to Southsea, Plymouth, to board with Captain Pryse Agar Holloway and his wife Mrs Sarah Holloway, a couple who cared for the children of couples born in British India. They were there for six years and Kipling would later recall their time there with horror, describing incidents of cruelty and neglect and wondering whether it was these which speeded up his literary maturity, for "it made me give attention to the lies I soon found it necessary to tell: and this, I presume, is the foundation of literary effort".

Alice's time, by contrast, was relatively comfortable, Mrs Holloway hoping that she would marry her son, though this ambition would not come to fruition. They did have relatives in England, a maternal aunt Georgiana and her husband who lived in Fulham, London, in a house at which they spent a month each Christmas and which Kipling later described as "a paradise which I verily believe saved me". Their mother returned in 1877 and removed them from their custody with the Holloways. A year later he gained admission to the United Services College at Westward Ho! in Devon, a recently established school with the intention of readying boys for military service in the British Army. His time here was fraught physically, though emotionally it proved fruitful for he began several firm friendships with other boys at the school. Moreover, he found in it inspiration for the setting of his series of schoolboy stories, Stalky and Co, begun in 1899. Meanwhile, his sister Alice had returned to Southsea and was boarding with Florence Garrard, with whom he fell in love and on whom he modeled Maisie in his first novel, The Light That Failed, published in 1891. At sixteen he was found lacking in the academic perspicacity necessary to undertake a scholarship to Oxford University, his parents meanwhile lacking the wherewithal to finance him therein. As such his father sought a job for him in Lahore, Punjab, where he was now a museum curator. The position he found for his son was as assistant editor of the Civil and Military Gazette, a small local newspaper. Kipling left for India on 20th September 1882, arriving in Bombay on 18th October. "There were yet three or four days" rail to Lahore, where my people lived. After these, my English years fell away, nor ever, I think, came back in full strength".

The Gazette appeared six days of the week, year-round save for a short break at both Christmas and Easter. Its editor Stephen Wheeler was diligent but Kipling's writing was insatiable, and he came to consider the paper his "mistress and most true love". In the summer of 1883 Kipling visited Shimla, the colonial hill-station and summer capital of British India which was then called Simla. Chosen by the British owing to its resemblance of English climate and scenery (as far as was possible in India), it became the seat of the Viceroy of India for the six months on the plains which were too hot for the British temperament, and subsequently became a "centre of power as well as pleasure". Lockwood was asked to serve in the Church there, and his family became yearly visitors while Kipling himself would take his annual leave here from 1885-88. The value of this time is evident from the regularity with which Simla appears in his writing for the Gazette, which in his journals he describes the time as

"....pure joy—every golden hour counted. It began in heat and discomfort, by rail and road. It ended in the cool evening, with a wood fire in one's bedroom, and next morn—thirty more of them ahead!—the early cup of tea, the Mother who brought it in, and the long talks of us all together again."

In 1886, his Departmental Ditties appeared, his first collection of verse, and brought with it a change of editor; Kay Robinson, Wheeler's replacement, was in favour of Kipling's creativity and granted him more freedom in that respect, even asking him to write short stories to appear in the newspaper. The vivacity of his writing was captured in a description of him by an ex-colleague at the Gazette, saying he "never knew such a fellow for ink—he simply revelled in it, filling up his pen viciously, and then throwing the contents all over the office, so that it was almost dangerous to approach him". While in Lahore, he had thirty-nine stories published in the Gazette between November 1886 and June 1887. Most of these are compiled in Plain Tales from the Hills, his first collection of prose, which was published in January 1888 in Calcutta, shortly after his 22nd birthday. In November 1887, he transferred from the Gazette to its much larger sister newspaper, The Pioneer, based in Allahabad. The pace of his writing remained, and in 1888 he published six collections of stories, Soldiers Three, The Story of the Gadsbys, In Black and White, Under the Deodars, The Phantom Rickshaw and Wee Willie Winkie, composed of some 41 stories. In addition, his position as The Pioneer's special correspondent in the Western region of Rajputna, he wrote many sketches which were later compiled in Letters of Marque and published in From Sea to Sea and Other Sketches, Letters of Travel.

A dispute in 1889 saw him discharged from The Pioneer, though by now he had been considering his future and sold the rights to his six volumes of stories for £200 and a small royalty, while the Plain Tales fetched £50, along with six months' salary from The Pioneer in lieu of notice. Using the money to undertake a pilgrimage to London, the literary centre of the British Empire, he left India on 9th March 1889, travelling via Rangoon, San Francisco, Hong Kong and Japan, then through the United States writing articles for The Pioneer which were also included in From Sea to Sea and Other Sketches, Letters of Travel. Arriving in England at Liverpool on October 1889, London and his literary début there beckoned.

His first task was to find a place to live, and he eventually settled on quarters in Villiers Street, Strand. The next two years saw several stories accepted by various magazine editors, the publication of the novel The Light That Failed, a nervous breakdown, the collaboration with Wolcott Balestier on the novel (uncharacterstically misspelt) The Naulhaka, and in 1891, following his doctors' advice, he embarked on a further sea voyage, travelling to South Africa, Australia, New Zealand and also returning to India. His plans to spend Christmas with his family were cut short on the news of Balestier's sudden death from typhoid fever, prompting an immediate return to London. Before he left, he had proposed to Balestier's sister Caroline Starr Balestier, with whom he had been having a hushed romance for just over a year. Back in London, Life's Handicap was published in 1891, a collection of short stories whose subject was the British in India, and British India. On 18th January 1892 aged 26 he married Caroline in the midst of an epidemic of influenza. Caroline was given away by Henry James, the famous and celebrated American author.

Honeymooning in Japan, they travelled via Vermont, America, to visit the Balestier estate, and upon arrival in Yokahama they found that their bank, The New Oriental Banking Corporation, had failed, though this loss did not deter them and they returned to Vermont, Caroline now pregnant with their first child. Renting a cottage on a farm for $10 per month, they lived a spartan existence and were "extraordinarily and self-centredly content". The named the residence Bliss Cottage, and it was here that the child was born, named Josephine, "in three foot of snow on the night of 29th December 1892. Her Mother's birthday being the 31st and mine the 30th we congratulated her on her sense of the fitness of things." While here, Kipling had his first ideas for the Jungle Books. Shortly after Josephine was born the couple moved in pursuit of more space and comfort, buying ten acres overlooking the Connecticut

River from Caroline's brother. The house they built there was inspired by the Mughul architecture he encountered in Lahore, and was named Naulakha (this time correctly spelt) in honour of Wolcott. His literary output in four years here included the Jungle Books, a collection of short stories entitled The Day's Work, the novel Captain Courageous and a plethora of poetry, of which most notably the volume The Seven Seas and his Barrack-Room Ballads. Meanwhile, he enjoyed correspondence with the many children who wrote to him about the Jungle Books.

In between this writing, Kipling took regular visitors. Most notably Arthur Conan Doyle came, bringing golf clubs and staying for two days to give Kipling an extended golf lesson. Kipling enjoyed the game so much that he continued to play, even in winter with special red balls, though he found that the ice would lead to drives travelling two miles as they slid "down the long slope to the Connecticut River". Elsie, the couple's second daughter, was born in February 1896, and by this time it is thought that their marriage had lost its original spark of spontaneity and descended into routine, though they remained loyal to one another. By now, failed arbitration between the United States and England over a border dispute involving British Guiana incited Anglo-American tensions which, in May 1896, resulted in a confrontation between Kipling and Caroline's brother, resulting in his arrest and, in the hearing which followed, the destruction of Kipling's private life, leaving him exhausted and miserable and leading to their return to England.

They had settled Torquay, Devon, by September 1896, and he remained socially present and literarily productive. The success of his writing had brought him fame, and he had responded with a sense of duty to include in his writing elements of political persuasion, most notably in his two poems Recessional and The White Man's Burden, which caused controversy when they were published in 1897 and 1899 respectively. Many considered them anthemic to the empire, propaganda for the imperial mindset so prevalent in the Victoria era. Their first son, John, was born in August 1887. Another journey to South Africa began a tradition of wintering there, which continued until 1908. His reputation as Poet of the Empire saw him well-received by politicians in the Cape Colony, and he started the newspaper The Friend for Lord Roberts and the British troops in Bloemfontein. Back in England, they moved to Rottingdean, East Sussex, in 1897, and in 1902 he bought Bateman's, a house built in 1630, which was his home from until his death in 1936. Kim was published in 1902, after which he collected material for Just So Stories for Little Children, published a year later. Both he and Josephine developed pneumonia while visiting the United States, from which she later died.

This decade proved his most successful, being awarded the Nobel Prize for Literature in 1907, the prize citation reading "in consideration of the power of observation, originality of imagination, virility of ideas and remarkable talent for narration which characterise the creations of this world-famous author". He was the first English-language recipient. At the award ceremony in Switzerland, Carl David af Wirsén praised Kipling and the English literary tradition:

> The Swedish Academy, in awarding the Nobel Prize in Literature this year to Rudyard Kipling, desires to pay a tribute to the literature of England, so rich in manifold glories, and to the greatest genius in the realm of narrative that that country has produced in our times.

Following this achievement, Kipling published Rewards and Fairies, which contained If, voted Britain's favourite poem in a BBC opinion poll in 1995. He turned down several recommendations for knighthood and was considered for Poet Laureate, though this position was never offered to him.

The sense of perseverance, honour and stoicism in If prevailed in many of his opinions, including that on the First World War. Writing in The New Army in Training in 1915, he scorned those who refused conscription, considering

> ....what will be the position in years to come of the young man who has deliberately elected to outcaste himself from this all-embracing brotherhood? What of his family, and, above all, what of his descendants, when the books have been closed and the last balance struck of sacrifice and sorrow in every hamlet, village, parish, suburb, city, shire, district, province, and Dominion throughout the Empire?

This attitude saw him encourage his son, John, to go to war, and he was promptly killed at the Battle of Loos in September 1915, aged 18. Last seen during the battle stumbling blindly through the mud, screaming in agony after an exploding shell had ripped his face apart, Kipling would write—

"If any question why we died
Tell them, because our fathers lied"

—perhaps betraying the guilt he felt at encouraging his son to go to war and finding him a position in the Irish Guards through his friendship with commander-in-chief Lord Roberts, for whom he had established The Friend in Bloemfontein. His death inspired much of Kipling's successive writing, notably My Boy Jack and a two-volume history of the Irish Guards, considered one of the finest examples of regimental history. Ironically, though his writing and his political position had arguably cost John his life, after the war he became friends with a French soldier whose copy of Kim, kept in his breast pocket, had stopped a bullet and saved his life. For a while the book and the soldier's Croix de Guerre were with Kipling, presented as tokens of gratitude, and they remained in contact, though when Kipling learned of the soldier's child he insisted on returning both book and medal.

He kept writing until 1930, though at a considerably slower pace, and to less success. His death, already once incorrectly announced early by a magazine in a premature obituary (and to which he responded "I've just read that I am dead. Don't forget to delete me from your list of subscribers") came on 18th January 1936, at the age of 70, from a perforated duodenal ulcer. His coffin was carried by, among others, his cousin the Prime Minister Stanley Baldwin, and his marble casket covered by a Union flag. He was cremated at Golders Green Crematorium in Northwest London and his ashes are buried at Poets' Corner in Westminster Abbey, alongside the graves of both Charles Dickens and Thomas Hardy.

In conjunction with various earthly memorials which commemorate him, alongside his extensive writing, he has a crater on Mercury named after him. The question of memorial and monument is much-addressed in English Literature and, as various great authors and poets have agreed before Kipling's time, his memory lives on more vivaciously set in his words, far longer and better represented than it could set in stone.

Rudyard Kipling - A Concise Bibliography

Books
The City of Dreadful Night (1885, short story)
Plain Tales from the Hills (1888)

Soldiers Three (1888)
The Story of the Gadsbys (1888)
In Black and White (1888)
Under the Deodars (1888)
The Phantom 'Rickshaw and other Eerie Tales (1888)
Wee Willie Winkie and Other Child Stories (1888)
Life's Handicap (1891)
The Light that Failed (1891) (novel)
American Notes (1891) (non-fiction)
The Naulahka: A Story of West and East (1892) (with Wolcott Balestie)
Many Inventions (1893)
The Jungle Book (1894)
Mowgli's Brothers (short story)
Kaa's Hunting (short story)
Tiger! Tiger! (short story)
The White Seal (short story)
Rikki-Tikki-Tavi (short story)
Toomai of the Elephants (short story)
Her Majesty's Servants (originally titled Servants of the Queen) (short story)
The Second Jungle Book (1895)
How Fear Came (short story)
The Miracle of Purun Bhagat (short story)
Letting in the Jungle (short story)
The Undertakers (short story)
The King's Ankus (short story)
Quiquern (short story)
Red Dog" (short story)
The Spring Running (short story)
Captains Courageous (1896) (novel)
The Day's Work (1898)
A Fleet in Being (1898)
Stalky & Co. (1899)
From Sea to Sea and Other Sketches, Letters of Travel (1899) (non-fiction)
Kim (1901) (novel)
Just So Stories for Little Children (1902)
Traffics and Discoveries (1904) (24 collected short stories)
With the Night Mail (1905) A Story of 2000 A.D
Puck of Pook's Hill (1906)
The Brushwood Boy (1907)
Actions and Reactions (1909)
A Song of the English (1909) (with W. Heath Robinson illustrator)
Rewards and Fairies (1910)
A History of England (1911) (non-fiction with Charles Robert Leslie Fletcher)
Songs from Books (1912)
As Easy as A.B.C. (1912) (Science-fiction short story)
The Fringes of the Fleet (1915) (non-fiction)
Sea Warfare (1916) (non-fiction)
A Diversity of Creatures (1917)

Land and Sea Tales for Scouts and Guides (1923)
The Irish Guards in the Great War (1923) (non-fiction)
Debits and Credits (1926)
A Book of Words (1928) (non-fiction)
Thy Servant a Dog (1930)
Limits and Renewals (1932)
Tales of India: the Windermere Series (1935)
Something of Myself (1937) (autobiography)
The Elephant's Child (fiction)

Autobiographies and Speeches
A Book of Words (1928)
Something of Myself (1937)

Short Story Collections
Quartette (1885) – with his father, mother, and sister
Plain Tales from the Hills (1888)
Soldiers Three, The Story of the Gadsbys, In Black and White (1888)
The Phantom 'Rickshaw and other Eerie Tales (1888)
Under the Deodars (1888)
Wee Willie Winkie and Other Child Stories (1888)
Life's Handicap (1891)
Many Inventions (1893)
The Jungle Book (1894)
The Second Jungle Book (1895)
The Day's Work (1898)
Life's Handicap (1899)
Stalky & Co. (1899)
Just So Stories (1902)
Traffics and Discoveries (1904)
Puck of Pook's Hill (1906)
Actions and Reactions (1909)
Abaft the Funnel (1909)
Rewards and Fairies (1910)
The Eyes of Asia (1917)
A Diversity of Creatures (1917)
Land and Sea Tales for Scouts and Guides (1923)
Debits and Credits (1926)
Thy Servant a Dog (1930)
Limits and Renewals (1932)

Military Collections
A Fleet in Being (1898)
France at War (1915)
The New Army in Training (1915)

Sea Warfare (1916)
The War in the Mountains (1917)
The Graves of the Fallen (1919)
The Irish Guards in the Great War (1923)

Poetry Collections
Schoolboy Lyrics (1881)
Echoes (1884) – with his sister, Alice ('Trix')
Departmental Ditties (1886)
Barrack-Room Ballads (1890)
The Seven Seas (1896)
An Almanac of Twelve Sports (1898, with illustrations by William Nicholson)
The Five Nations (1903)
Collected Verse (1907)
Songs from Books (1912)
The Years Between (1919)
Rudyard Kipling's Verse: Definitive Edition (1940)
The Muse Among the Motors (poetry)

Travel Writing
From Sea to Sea – Letters of Travel: 1887–1889 (1899)
Letters of Travel: 1892–1913 (1920)
Souvenirs of France (1933)
Brazilian Sketches: 1927 (1940)

Collected Works
The Outward Bound Edition (1897–1937, 36 volumes)
The Edition de Luxe (1897–1937, 38 volumes)
The Bombay Edition (1913–38, 31 volumes)
The Sussex Edition (1937–39, 35 volumes)
The Burwash Edition (1941, 28 volumes)

Poems
Departmental Ditties and Other Verses (1886)
Barrack Room Ballads (1889, republished with additions at later times)
The Seven Seas and Further Barrack-Room Ballads (In various editions 1891–96)
The Five Nations (with some new and some reprinted and revised poems, 1903)
Twenty-two original 'Historical Poems' (1911)
Songs from Books (1912)
The Years Between (1919)

Posthumous Collections
Rudyard Kipling's Verse: Definitive edition

A Choice of Kipling's Verse, edited by T.S. Eliot

In addition Kipling wrote and published many hundreds of poems too numerous to include here.